The
Productivity
Habit

Interior and Cover Designer: Richard Tapp
Art Producer: Sue Smith
Editor: Justin Hartung
Production Manager: Jose Olivera
Production Editor: Erum Khan
ISBN: 978-1-64152-902-0
R0

The Productivity Habit

A 10-Week Journal to Become More Productive

Cathy Sexton

ROCKRIDGE
PRESS

Introduction

We all have a lot to accomplish each day, and there are only so many hours in a day to get things done. As we're running the race against time to get it all done, many of us struggle with making sure we take care of ourselves, devote enough time to important relationships, and make the most of this life we're each living. Trying to juggle it all can be overwhelming, but it doesn't need to be! Improving our ability to be truly productive changes the game.

Too many of us get caught in the trap of thinking that working harder and putting in longer hours is how you get more done and achieve success. I can tell you from personal experience, that's not a healthy way to live. I've lived that lifestyle, and I ran myself into the ground trying to do it all and have it all. As a result, I was diagnosed with Graves' Disease, a stress-induced, life-threatening autoimmune disorder.

Facing my health crisis was a difficult and scary time, but what I learned through that experience changed my life for the better. It forced me to re-evaluate my values, goals, and habits. I learned to work smarter, not harder. It also led to my mission of helping others develop healthier work and life habits, so they can excel in their work life and balance it all with quality time for the people and things that matter most in their personal life, too.

Healthy habits, beliefs, and behaviors are at the heart of productivity and creating a balanced, more productive life. They are the foundation for successfully juggling and balancing it all. The decisions you make about what you will focus your time and energy on every single day impact your ability to achieve your goals and dreams. The question is, what are you basing those decisions on? Sometimes we don't even know. Our choices can be dictated by a mindset and/or beliefs we're not even aware of. In those cases, insight and clarity allow us to make more intentional choices, which has a powerful, positive impact on productivity and our lives overall.

I want that powerful, positive impact for you.

As you work your way through this journal, there may be times you find yourself wondering, "What does this have to do with productivity?" Just trust me. It all matters. The concepts and principles I'm sharing here reflect more than 16 years of helping individuals and business owners ignite their productivity so they can get more done in less time, and with less stress. It's all part of making smaller changes which will consistently bring better results, both now and in the future. There's a bigger picture to the productivity puzzle, and you're about to start putting the pieces in place.

How to Use
This Journal

There are plenty of "do this" or "do that" tips for getting things done more efficiently, but the fact that many of us still struggle indicates productivity and success are about more than just simple tips. Implementing one-off tips and "life hacks" may help in the short-term, but it's like putting a Band-Aid on a wound that needs stitches. There are roadblocks to productivity that can keep you from successfully making the changes you want and need to make. When you address those roadblocks, you make changes which are meaningful, lasting, and actually fix the issues you're dealing with.

This journal is designed to help you do just that. Reflecting, evaluating, and "thinking on paper" are valuable tools in the process. Combining a deep dive into what's holding you back with positive action will bring the results you want to see, even if those results have eluded you in the past.

As you go through the next 10 weeks, you'll be keeping your goal of greater productivity at the top of your mind, while making conscious choices about the daily and weekly changes you want to make. Why 10 weeks? It's the perfect amount of time to get you solidly on the path to change that lasts, and it takes maintaining new habits and actions you put in place to a whole new level.

Each week, you'll find a series of five Daily Prompts, which are designed to get you thinking about the roadblocks that may be keeping you from the success you desire and provide space to write out your thoughts. Take your time, reflect, and answer each prompt as honestly as you can. Once you've completed the daily prompt, you'll see a corresponding Goal Setting page where you will define how to turn your insight into action and implement those actions. It's important to note that this page can be used in different ways: You can set a new goal every day or use it to create micro-goals that move you closer toward a larger goal you're working toward.

On the sixth day of each week, you'll find a weekly Habit Tracker page, which will encourage you to reflect on your insights and progress from the previous week. Each of these also includes a Power-Up! tip designed to boost your efforts and get you in the mindset of rewarding yourself for a week of effort and progress. Getting in the habit of doing something special for yourself at the end of a productive week is a great strategy for ongoing success.

The seventh day each week is an "off" day. Taking that seventh day off allows you to enjoy some well-deserved rest and relaxation, so you can refresh and recharge after working to become more productive throughout the week.

Finally, you'll find Make It a Habit tips sprinkled throughout the journal. These smaller actionable tips and tools for working more efficiently can be incorporated into your life right away and will help you in your journey of living your best, most productive life.

This combination of reflection and insight, goal setting, tips, and action is a comprehensive approach to creating better habits and getting results. You'll uncover what might be holding you back and have the insight you need to make real changes. It's all designed to help you break through roadblocks and increase your productivity in a way you've never experienced before.

The Five Roadblocks
to Productivity

What's holding you back from being more productive? There are a number of potential roadblocks to productivity, but they all tend to fall within five key areas that have a huge impact on your ability to be productive and successful. Each of these roadblocks are the areas in which we are looking to make changes so that you are able to jump right onto the path to being more productive. Let's dive into those five roadblocks and some examples.

MINDSET

Our mindset is perhaps the most important of all the road-blocks, as it consists of our own conscious and subconscious beliefs about what we can or cannot do. Those beliefs about ourselves skew our view of the world around us—both positively and negatively—and affect every aspect of our lives and businesses. They influence how we choose to use our time. They affect our ability to clarify what we want and why. They also impact our ability to dream big, which prompts us to set goals for the future. Basically, if our mindset and beliefs are limiting, our potential will be limited, too.

PLANNING

It's been said that a goal is really just a wish if it lacks an intentional path you can follow to achieve it. That makes planning a critical piece of the productivity puzzle. It helps you break larger goals into manageable steps and milestones that keep the goal right in front of you, which provides motivation to keep moving forward. Planning helps keep you on track, and it can also shed light on potential obstacles.

PRIORITIZATION

Anyone can look at a list of to-dos and decide to do one task over another. That's the easy part. The challenge comes in knowing which tasks should be prioritized. Determining what tasks fit with your vision and goals can be the difference between success and failure. Prioritization helps you be intentional with the tasks you choose to invest your valuable time and energy in versus just being busy.

FOCUS

Focus helps you make the most of the time you spend working on tasks. Learning what to focus on and how to be more intentional with your time is the key to working smarter rather than harder. Distractions and interruptions, a cluttered work environment, and unproductive daily habits can all shift focus away from what truly matters and keep you stuck, while planning and prioritizing both play a positive role in helping you get focused on the right things each day.

ENERGY

Your ability to do everything you need to do depends heavily on your energy level. Productivity can either flourish or fizzle based on the pace you set. If you're overwhelmed, overworked, or stressed and trying to function without enough rest, your productivity will suffer. Your mind and body simply won't have what they need to fuel your efforts.

Overcoming these five roadblocks starts with taking an honest look at where you currently stand, then making adjustments and creating healthier habits in areas where you may be struggling. In doing that, you'll align your mindset and actions for greater results. You'll find yourself focusing on what really matters and getting more done in less time, and with less stress. You'll also be on your way to actually achieving the goals you set, and that's the ultimate goal. So let's get started!

This Book Belongs To:

NAME

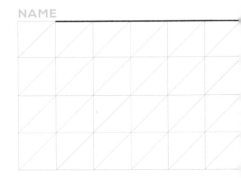

▨ I WANT TO BE MORE PRODUCTIVE WHEN I:

The Importance of Being Honest: A Place to Start

As you begin your journey to greater productivity, it's important to reflect on where you are. Start by taking an honest look at where you're struggling and where you would like to see improvement. When you consider Mindset, Planning, Prioritizing, Focus, and Energy, what are your weakest points and greatest challenges?

■ **MINDSET:**

_____

_____

■ **PLANNING:**

_____

_____

■ **PRIORITIZING:**

_____

_____

■ **FOCUS:**

_____

_____

■ **ENERGY:**

_____

_____

GOAL SETTING

Setting goals in the areas of Mindset, Planning, Prioritizing, Focus, and Energy helps you fully incorporate healthier habits and productivity principles into your life. Think about how each principle on the previous page applies to your life, then use this page to set a goal and define the action steps you will take to keep moving forward.

▪ **MY GOAL IS:**

_____

_____

▪ **I WILL REACH MY GOAL BY THIS DATE:**

_____

▪ **IS THERE A DAILY, WEEKLY, OR MONTHLY ACTION I CAN TAKE?**

_____

_____

▪ **MY ACTION STEP(S):**

_____

_____

▪ **WHAT WILL REMIND ME TO KEEP MOVING FORWARD? :**

_____

_____

How Willing Are You to Make Some Changes?

Change can be difficult for some. It requires consistent, intentional decisions to adopt new habits. Honestly assessing your willingness to embrace new habits and behaviors is one of the first steps to making changes that will increase your productivity. What might hold you back from changing old habits and implementing the new for a more productive life?

■ **WHAT HABIT(S) HAVE I BEEN SUCCESSFUL AT CHANGING?**

_____

_____

_____

■ **WHAT HABITS HAVE I TRIED TO CHANGE WITHOUT SUCCESS?**

_____

_____

_____

■ **WHAT COULD BE HOLDING ME BACK FROM MAKING THE CHANGES I DESIRE?**

_____

_____

_____

_____

GOAL SETTING

■ **MY GOAL IS:**

_____

_____

■ **I WILL REACH MY GOAL BY THIS DATE:**

_____

_____

■ **IS THERE A DAILY, WEEKLY, OR MONTHLY ACTION I CAN TAKE?**

_____

_____

_____

■ **MY ACTION STEP(S):**

_____

_____

_____

■ **WHAT WILL REMIND ME TO KEEP MOVING FORWARD?**

_____

_____

Understanding What's Holding You Back

Are you easily distracted? Maybe you're a big-idea person who gets bogged down by details and struggles to plan and prioritize. Maybe you feel overwhelmed or burned out by days that spin out of control. All of these things (and more) affect productivity and keep you from achieving goals.

DESCRIBE WHAT YOU BELIEVE HAS BEEN HOLDING YOU BACK FROM BEING MORE PRODUCTIVE.

(e.g., I'm overwhelmed by too much to do and it all seems important, interruptions, stress, low energy, or something else.)

_____

_____

_____

_____

_____

_____

_____

_____

_____

_____

_____

GOAL SETTING

■ **MY GOAL IS:**

_____

_____

■ **I WILL REACH MY GOAL BY THIS DATE:**

_____

_____

■ **IS THERE A DAILY, WEEKLY, OR MONTHLY ACTION I CAN TAKE?**

_____

_____

_____

■ **MY ACTION STEP(S):**

_____

_____

_____

■ **WHAT WILL REMIND ME TO KEEP MOVING FORWARD?**

_____

_____

Are You Afraid You'll Fail or Afraid You'll Succeed?

We're all familiar with fear of failure, but have you ever considered you might be just as afraid of success? Fear of success or failure can sabotage your potential to succeed. Making positive changes in our lives is a good thing, but sometimes we have to walk through our fears to get to our greatness. What are your fears around success and failure?

■ MY BELIEFS ABOUT SUCCESS:

_____

_____

_____

■ MY BELIEFS ABOUT FAILURE:

_____

_____

_____

■ MY GREATEST FEARS:

_____

_____

_____

_____

GOAL SETTING

▪ **MY GOAL IS:**

_____

_____

▪ **I WILL REACH MY GOAL BY THIS DATE:**

_____

_____

▪ **IS THERE A DAILY, WEEKLY, OR MONTHLY ACTION I CAN TAKE?**

_____

_____

_____

▪ **MY ACTION STEP(S):**

_____

_____

_____

▪ **WHAT WILL REMIND ME TO KEEP MOVING FORWARD?**

_____

_____

Are You Tired of Playing Whack-a-Mole?

If you're constantly busy but not productive, you can start to get discouraged or even burned out. You may feel like you're checking things off your to-do list, but you might just be playing whack-a-mole and constantly putting out fires. Reflect on where you stand in terms of the time you spend playing whack-a-mole and how that makes you feel at the end of the day.

■ **HOW MUCH TIME DO I SPEND REACTING VS. BEING INTENTIONAL WITH MY TIME AND ACTIONS?**

_____

_____

_____

■ **HOW DOES THAT MAKE ME FEEL?**

_____

_____

_____

■ **IN WHAT WAYS COULD I BE MORE INTENTIONAL WITH MY TIME?**

_____

_____

_____

_____

GOAL SETTING

■ **MY GOAL IS:**

_____

_____

■ **I WILL REACH MY GOAL BY THIS DATE:**

_____

_____

■ **IS THERE A DAILY, WEEKLY, OR MONTHLY ACTION I CAN TAKE?**

_____

_____

_____

■ **MY ACTION STEP(S):**

_____

_____

_____

■ **WHAT WILL REMIND ME TO KEEP MOVING FORWARD?**

_____

_____

HABIT TRACKER

Looking back over your journal for the past week, where would you say you stand right now in terms of what's been holding you back, your willingness to change, and your fears around changing habits? Also, was there anything you discovered that surprised you?

_____

_____

_____

_____

_____

_____

_____

_____

_____

_____

_____

_____

_____

_____

_____

_____

MAKE IT A HABIT

Stress and overwhelm are fairly common in today's busy world. Struggling to juggle it all can really take a toll on you physically and mentally. Make it a habit to start your days with some kind of "centering" ritual. Just 10 to 15 minutes at the start of the day could really make a difference in setting the tone for the rest of the day. It could be prayer, meditation, visualization with positive affirmations, or anything you choose that will work for you. Just start each day in a calm, focused, positive way.

POWER UP!

Hobbies can be great for helping you unplug from daily stressors, but with all you have going on, you may have been neglecting your favorite hobbies or activities you enjoy. Take some time today to enjoy a hobby or interest that nurtures you—guilt-free and without thinking about to-do lists.

Is Your Personality Style Affecting Your Productivity?

How does your personality style affect your productivity? Our personality traits affect how well we communicate, how quickly we make decisions, and whether we jump right in with gusto or procrastinate until the last minute. Traits can also affect whether details drive you crazy or make you smile—among other things. Are there aspects of your personality that help or hinder you? Reflect on which parts of your personality might be affecting your productivity and why.

■ **TRAITS WITH A POSITIVE EFFECT:**

_____

_____

_____

_____

_____

_____

■ **TRAITS WITH A NEGATIVE EFFECT:**

_____

_____

_____

_____

_____

_____

GOAL SETTING

■ MY GOAL IS:

_____

_____

■ I WILL REACH MY GOAL BY THIS DATE:

_____

_____

■ IS THERE A DAILY, WEEKLY, OR MONTHLY ACTION I
CAN TAKE?

_____

_____

_____

■ MY ACTION STEP(S):

_____

_____

_____

■ WHAT WILL REMIND ME TO KEEP MOVING FORWARD?

_____

_____

Mindset
Moving Forward

We all can have unhealthy beliefs about ourselves, our worth, and our potential playing in our minds. These negative messages can come from comments made by others or experiences we've had in our life, linger in our subconscious mind, and sabotage our potential. We often accept them as true, though they rarely are. Fortunately, we have the power and ability to change the negative beliefs to healthier, more positive messages by identifying them, acknowledging them, and making a conscious effort to change them. Write out any negative messages that play in your mind, then reframe them into the positive messages that reflect what's really true.

■ **THE NEGATIVE MESSAGES THAT RUN THROUGH MY MIND ARE . . .**
(e.g., I never finish what I start, I don't manage my time or money well, I'm too "flighty" to run a successful business or be good at my job, I'm not smart enough)

_____

_____

_____

■ **THE TRUTH IS . . .**
(e.g., I am capable of success, I am responsible with my time and money, I am good at my job, I am capable of learning new things)

_____

_____

_____

_____

GOAL SETTING

■ MY GOAL IS:

_____
_____

■ I WILL REACH MY GOAL BY THIS DATE:

_____
_____

■ IS THERE A DAILY, WEEKLY, OR MONTHLY ACTION I
CAN TAKE?

_____
_____
_____

■ MY ACTION STEP(S):

_____
_____
_____

■ WHAT WILL REMIND ME TO KEEP MOVING FORWARD?

_____
_____

Striking the Right Balance

We should never be so busy building a life and future that we forget to live and enjoy our life right now. Even if you love the work you do, a balance between work and other things is so important! Our drive to succeed can cause us to lose sight of that. How strong is your drive to succeed, and how is that affecting balance in your life? How can you create a better work-life balance?

_____

_____

_____

_____

_____

_____

_____

_____

_____

_____

_____

_____

_____

_____

_____

GOAL SETTING

■ MY GOAL IS:

_____

_____

■ I WILL REACH MY GOAL BY THIS DATE:

_____

_____

■ IS THERE A DAILY, WEEKLY, OR MONTHLY ACTION I CAN TAKE?

_____

_____

_____

■ MY ACTION STEP(S):

_____

_____

_____

■ WHAT WILL REMIND ME TO KEEP MOVING FORWARD?

_____

_____

What Do You Value Most?

When you let your values guide your decisions, you create a life you value. What do you value most? Your work? Your family? Your health? Honesty, integrity, and reputation? Take a few minutes to write about what you value most in your life and how well you feel you are honoring those values.

■ **WHAT DO I VALUE MOST IN MY LIFE?**

_____

_____

_____

_____

_____

_____

■ **HOW WELL AM I HONORING THOSE VALUES, AND WHAT NEEDS TO CHANGE TO BETTER REFLECT WHAT I VALUE?**

_____

_____

_____

_____

_____

_____

GOAL SETTING

- **MY GOAL IS:**

_____

_____

- **I WILL REACH MY GOAL BY THIS DATE:**

_____

_____

- **IS THERE A DAILY, WEEKLY, OR MONTHLY ACTION I CAN TAKE?**

_____

_____

_____

- **MY ACTION STEP(S):**

_____

_____

_____

- **WHAT WILL REMIND ME TO KEEP MOVING FORWARD?**

_____

_____

The Difference Between Busyness and Productivity

There is a difference between busyness and productivity. It is possible to be extremely busy, yet not truly productive. We often get caught up in tasks that aren't important in terms of reaching our goals or moving a project forward, because we're not consciously planning and prioritizing. When we get stuck in this cycle, days (even weeks) can fly by without making progress toward our goals. How does busyness versus productivity apply in your life or business, and how well are you handling decisions about how you spend your time and what should be prioritized each day?

■ **HOW DOES BEING BUSY VERSUS BEING PRODUCTIVE APPLY IN MY LIFE OR BUSINESS?**
(e.g., how often do days spin out of control, how well are you prioritizing tasks)

_____

_____

_____

_____

■ **WHAT SYSTEM COULD I USE TO BE BETTER AT PRIORITIZING TASKS TO MAKE SURE THE THINGS I'M DOING ARE PRODUCTIVE AND IN LINE WITH MY GOALS?**
(e.g., be more intentional, plan on Sunday night for the week ahead)

_____

_____

_____

GOAL SETTING

■ MY GOAL IS:

_____

_____

■ I WILL REACH MY GOAL BY THIS DATE:

_____

_____

■ IS THERE A DAILY, WEEKLY, OR MONTHLY ACTION I
CAN TAKE?

_____

_____

_____

■ MY ACTION STEP(S):

_____

_____

_____

■ WHAT WILL REMIND ME TO KEEP MOVING FORWARD?

_____

_____

HABIT TRACKER

With what you've discovered about yourself and your productivity so far, how would you say your habits and behaviors have contributed to the five roadblocks to productivity?

■ MINDSET:

_____

■ PLANNING:

_____

■ PRIORITIZING:

_____

■ FOCUS:

_____

■ ENERGY:

_____

MAKE IT A HABIT

To-do lists are great for directing your activities each day; just make-sure your lists are written as tasks and not results. For example, if you were writing a book, instead of writing "finish first chapter," which is the result, you would break it down into the specific action steps instead, such as "proofread first chapter," "write 1,000 words," "research sources for chapter one," etc. Be specific and detailed. Break results into actionable task-bites, and you are more likely to dig in and get all your to-dos done.

POWER UP!

Treat yourself to a planner that will work for you and make your life easier. Pick something that will give you space for scheduling and daily tasks, but also some-thing that will give you space to dream and track your goals. Even if it initially feels like an unnecessary expense, think of it as an investment in you and your new path.

Defining Your Strengths and Weaknesses

We all have strengths and weaknesses. Being honest and clear about what yours are can be difficult, but it's an important piece of the productivity puzzle. Knowing your strengths helps you determine what you should do more of. Knowing your weaknesses helps you identify areas where you either need to learn more or turn the task over to someone who can do it better and faster. What do you see as your strengths and weaknesses in life or business?

■ MY STRENGTHS ARE:

_____

_____

■ MY WEAKNESSES ARE:

_____

_____

■ MY OPPORTUNITIES FOR USING MY STRENGTHS MORE ARE:

_____

_____

■ I COULD MINIMIZE OR FILL IN THE GAPS CAUSED BY MY WEAKNESSES BY:

_____

_____

GOAL SETTING

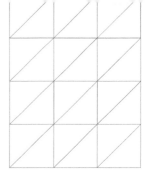

■ **MY GOAL IS:**

_____

_____

■ **I WILL REACH MY GOAL BY THIS DATE:**

_____

_____

■ **IS THERE A DAILY, WEEKLY, OR MONTHLY ACTION I CAN TAKE?**

_____

_____

_____

■ **MY ACTION STEP(S):**

_____

_____

_____

■ **WHAT WILL REMIND ME TO KEEP MOVING FORWARD?**

_____

_____

Is Your Mindset Helping or Holding You Back?

Scarcity or abundance. Bad attitude or gratitude. "I can't" versus "I can." Do you greet each day with a positive or negative outlook? A limited mindset restricts your potential. You are basically holding yourself back by seeing yourself as incapable of learning and improving, or seeing the glass as half empty. How would you describe yourself in terms of mindset?

■ IN TERMS OF MINDSET, I AM . . .

_____

_____

_____

■ MY MINDSET HELPS ME IN THE FOLLOWING WAYS:

_____

_____

_____

_____

■ MY MINDSET HOLDS ME BACK IN THE FOLLOWING WAYS:

_____

_____

_____

_____

GOAL SETTING

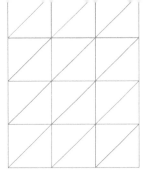

■ MY GOAL IS:

_____

_____

■ I WILL REACH MY GOAL BY THIS DATE:

_____

_____

■ IS THERE A DAILY, WEEKLY, OR MONTHLY ACTION I
  CAN TAKE?

_____

_____

_____

■ MY ACTION STEP(S):

_____

_____

_____

■ WHAT WILL REMIND ME TO KEEP MOVING FORWARD?

_____

_____

What's the Dream?

Gaining clarity about what you want for your future is an essential part of actually achieving it. After all, if you don't know where you're going, how will you ever get there? You can have goals in terms of productivity, but you should also have goals and dreams for your business or other areas of your life. What are your goals and dreams? (Describe in as much detail as possible.)

■ MY BIGGEST DREAM FOR MY CAREER IS:

_____

_____

_____

_____

_____

_____

■ MY GOALS AND DREAMS FOR MY LIFE OUTSIDE OF WORK ARE:

_____

_____

_____

_____

_____

_____

GOAL SETTING

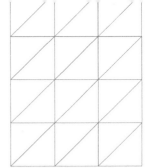

- **MY GOAL IS:**

_____

_____

- **I WILL REACH MY GOAL BY THIS DATE:**

_____

_____

- **IS THERE A DAILY, WEEKLY, OR MONTHLY ACTION I CAN TAKE?**

_____

_____

_____

- **MY ACTION STEP(S):**

_____

_____

_____

- **WHAT WILL REMIND ME TO KEEP MOVING FORWARD?**

_____

_____

Are You Wearing Too Many Hats?

How many hats are you wearing to get everything done? You only have so much energy each day to devote to tasks, so it's important to intentionally direct your energy to where it will be most benefi-cial. What are all of the hats you're wearing, and what could you delegate, outsource, ask for help with, or just let go of so you could really devote your precious energy to the things that matter most?

■ THE HATS I AM WEARING:

_____

_____

_____

_____

_____

_____

■ HATS I COULD DELEGATE, OUTSOURCE, ASK FOR HELP WITH, OR JUST LET GO OF:

_____

_____

_____

_____

_____

_____

GOAL SETTING

■ MY GOAL IS:

_____

_____

■ I WILL REACH MY GOAL BY THIS DATE:

_____

_____

■ IS THERE A DAILY, WEEKLY, OR MONTHLY ACTION I
CAN TAKE?

_____

_____

_____

■ MY ACTION STEP(S):

_____

_____

_____

■ WHAT WILL REMIND ME TO KEEP MOVING FORWARD?

_____

_____

The Value of "No": Setting Boundaries on Life Clutter

Is it hard for you to say "no" to requests, even when you know saying "yes" will increase your stress level and take time away from other things you'd rather do or should be doing? Have you ever wondered why you say yes anyway? Saying yes may help others but hurt your overall productivity, and it is important to place a high value on your own time and needs. Take a few minutes to reflect on why you say "yes" when you know deep down the answer should be "no."

■ **STRATEGIES FOR CHANGING THIS BEHAVIOR:**
   (e.g., delaying response until you check your schedule, having an accountability partner you run things by first)

_____

_____

_____

_____

_____

_____

_____

_____

_____

_____

_____

_____

GOAL SETTING

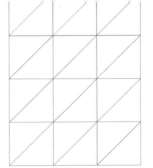

■ MY GOAL IS:

_____

_____

■ I WILL REACH MY GOAL BY THIS DATE:

_____

_____

■ IS THERE A DAILY, WEEKLY, OR MONTHLY ACTION I
CAN TAKE?

_____

_____

_____

■ MY ACTION STEP(S):

_____

_____

_____

■ WHAT WILL REMIND ME TO KEEP MOVING FORWARD?

_____

_____

HABIT TRACKER

Over the past couple of weeks, you've taken an honest look at how mindset and habits have affected your productivity and potential up to this point. It's often very empowering to realize things you were doing and choices you were making (sometimes without even being aware you were making them) are within your power to change. What are the biggest revelations you've had so far? How are you feeling about what you've uncovered and the possibility of making meaningful changes?

_____

_____

_____

_____

_____

_____

_____

_____

_____

_____

_____

_____

_____

_____

_____

_____

_____

MAKE IT A HABIT

Each day, choose your most important (or most dreaded) task off your to-do list. Make that your Top Important Priority **(TIP)** for the day. Block off the first 90 minutes to work on that TIP. When the time is up and you get that finished (or at least make excellent progress), take a short break, then move onto the next most important task. At the end of the day, you'll see progress and feel great that you accomplished something so substantial!

POWER UP!

Hobbies can be great for helping you unplug from daily stressors, but with all you have going on, you may have been neglecting your favorite hobbies or activities you enjoy. Take some time today to enjoy a hobby or interest that nurtures you— guilt-free and without thinking about to-do lists.

Taming Life's Big and Little Distractions

Daily life comes with all kinds of distractions. Some we have control of, and some we don't. What would you say are the biggest distractions that keep you from being productive throughout your day? How do they affect your productivity? Are they typically self-inflicted or do others frequently dump their "emergencies" on you?

■ **WHAT ARE MY BIGGEST DISTRACTIONS?**

_____

_____

_____

_____

■ **HOW DO THEY AFFECT MY PRODUCTIVITY?**

_____

_____

_____

_____

■ **AM I CREATING MY OWN DISTRACTIONS OR AM I LETTING OTHERS DOMINATE MY TIME? HOW COULD I CHANGE THAT?**

_____

_____

_____

GOAL SETTING

■ MY GOAL IS:

_____

_____

■ I WILL REACH MY GOAL BY THIS DATE:

_____

_____

■ IS THERE A DAILY, WEEKLY, OR MONTHLY ACTION I
  CAN TAKE?

_____

_____

_____

■ MY ACTION STEP(S):

_____

_____

_____

■ WHAT WILL REMIND ME TO KEEP MOVING FORWARD?

_____

_____

Making the Most of Time

We only have so much time each day. How do you view and use your time? Do you see even five minutes as an opportunity to get something accomplished, or do you spend those minutes scrolling on social media? Are you always on time, or do you often overbook or lose track of time and run late? Do you dive right into projects, or put them off until the last minute? Think about how you view and manage your time. How could you use the valuable resource of time more efficiently? Are there ways you waste time, and what could you do to change that?

■ MY CURRENT VIEW AND USE OF TIME IS . . .

_____

_____

■ WAYS I SQUANDER TIME WITHOUT REALIZING OR DON'T MANAGE MY TIME WELL:

_____

_____

■ CHANGES I COULD MAKE TO USE MY TIME MORE EFFICIENTLY:

_____

_____

GOAL SETTING

■ MY GOAL IS:

_____

_____

■ I WILL REACH MY GOAL BY THIS DATE:

_____

_____

■ IS THERE A DAILY, WEEKLY, OR MONTHLY ACTION I
CAN TAKE?

_____

_____

_____

■ MY ACTION STEP(S):

_____

_____

_____

■ WHAT WILL REMIND ME TO KEEP MOVING FORWARD?

_____

_____

The Myth of Multitasking

Multitasking was once touted as the way to get more done. Today, we know productivity fizzles when we try to do too many things at once. It can take up to 20 minutes for your brain to fully shift when you move from task to task. That adds up to a lot of lost time over the course of days and weeks! What are your thoughts on multitasking and how can you be more present and focused in the moment and on your current task?

■ **WHAT ROLE HAS MULTITASKING PLAYED IN MY CURRENT OR PAST PRODUCTIVITY?**

_____

_____

_____

_____

■ **WHAT ARE THE WAYS I CAN BE MORE FOCUSED ON THE TASK AT HAND AND PRESENT IN THE MOMENT?**
(e.g., turning off notifications, not constantly checking emails)

_____

_____

_____

_____

GOAL SETTING

◼ MY GOAL IS:

_____

_____

◼ I WILL REACH MY GOAL BY THIS DATE:

_____

_____

◼ IS THERE A DAILY, WEEKLY, OR MONTHLY ACTION I
   CAN TAKE?

_____

_____

_____

◼ MY ACTION STEP(S):

_____

_____

_____

◼ WHAT WILL REMIND ME TO KEEP MOVING FORWARD?

_____

_____

How Well Are You Caring for You?

A big part of productivity is taking care of yourself both physically and mentally. When we meet the needs of our bodies and minds, we have the energy we need to do what needs to be done. Where do you feel you're lacking in self-care? What actions could you take to improve your energy by taking good care of yourself?

■ **WHERE I COULD USE IMPROVEMENT:**
(e.g., sleep, diet, taking time for yourself, activities you enjoy but have neglected, exercise/physical activity, relationships)

_____

_____

_____

_____

_____

■ **WAYS TO IMPROVE:**

_____

_____

_____

_____

_____

GOAL SETTING

■ MY GOAL IS:

_____

_____

■ I WILL REACH MY GOAL BY THIS DATE:

_____

_____

■ IS THERE A DAILY, WEEKLY, OR MONTHLY ACTION I
  CAN TAKE?

_____

_____

_____

■ MY ACTION STEP(S):

_____

_____

_____

■ WHAT WILL REMIND ME TO KEEP MOVING FORWARD?

_____

_____

The Gratitude Boost

Developing an attitude of gratitude and abundance is life changing. When you learn to see the world from the perspective of "My glass is half full" or "I'm just so happy I have a glass and there's something in it," you open the door to possibilities and more positive life experiences. Describe areas of your life where your mindset is more gloomy than grateful. Then make a list of what the positive opposite would be and post the positives where you will see them every day.

■ **AREAS OF MY LIFE WHERE I AM MORE GLOOMY THAN GRATEFUL:**

_____

_____

■ **HOW I COULD FLIP EACH ONE FROM GLOOMY TO GRATEFUL:**

_____

_____

■ **POSITIVE STATEMENTS FOR EACH TO BE USED FOR DAILY ENCOURAGEMENT:**
(e.g., I am so grateful I have food and shelter for my family)

_____

_____

_____

GOAL SETTING

■ MY GOAL IS:

_____

_____

■ I WILL REACH MY GOAL BY THIS DATE:

_____

_____

■ IS THERE A DAILY, WEEKLY, OR MONTHLY ACTION I
CAN TAKE?

_____

_____

_____

■ MY ACTION STEP(S):

_____

_____

_____

■ WHAT WILL REMIND ME TO KEEP MOVING FORWARD?

_____

_____

HABIT TRACKER

It's week four and you're doing great! What good habits have you learned about and started implementing that are already bringing positive results to your productivity journey?

■ MINDSET:

_____

_____

■ PLANNING:

_____

_____

■ PRIORITIZING:

_____

_____

■ FOCUS:

_____

_____

■ ENERGY:

_____

_____

MAKE IT A HABIT

Often there are lulls in our day when we have a little extra time and could do something small but aren't sure what that could be. Create and keep a running list of tasks you could do when you have 5 to 10 minutes to spare. It might be answering emails, phone calls, filing, decluttering, or anything you could knock out in that short amount of time. Put them on the five-minute list, and you'll be surprised how quickly and easily they all get done.

POWER UP!

Celebrate a week full of hustle, healthier habits, and hoorays by taking some well-deserved time to enjoy this life you're building. Schedule lunch, dinner, or just a get-together with someone you've been wanting to catch up with; block out the time, make it a top priority on your schedule, and ENJOY!

Prioritize and Balance

It's important to prioritize and balance all of the different parts of your life. Make sure you have categories on your calendar for everything that deserves or requires your time. Color-coding and time blocking are great strategies for that! What categories will you include in your calendar to be sure you're honoring a balance between all of the things on your calendar? What's a reasonable amount of time to devote to each category in a day or week to maintain balance?

■ **MY CATEGORIES AND THE TIME I WILL BLOCK-OUT/ DEVOTE TO EACH:**
(e.g., personal time—blue; family time—green; work—orange; networking—yellow; learning/skill building—purple)

_____

_____

_____

_____

_____

_____

_____

_____

_____

_____

_____

GOAL SETTING

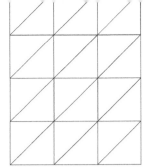

- **MY GOAL IS:**

_____

_____

- **I WILL REACH MY GOAL BY THIS DATE:**

_____

_____

- **IS THERE A DAILY, WEEKLY, OR MONTHLY ACTION I CAN TAKE?**

_____

_____

_____

- **MY ACTION STEP(S):**

_____

_____

_____

- **WHAT WILL REMIND ME TO KEEP MOVING FORWARD?**

_____

_____

Setting Boundaries to Guard Your Work Time

Others can intrude on your time and make demands that draw focus from your priorities. Adopt the mantra that your time is yours and it's valuable. It's okay to take control over what will and won't knock you off track, as only you can set those boundaries. How could you set effective boundaries to help others respect your time? The possibilities are endless, so get creative!

■ **TYPICAL INTRUSIONS ON MY DAY AND PRODUCTIVITY:**

_____

_____

_____

_____

■ **THE BOUNDARIES I COULD SET ARE . . .**
  (e.g., keeping your door shut while you're working, not providing a place for others to sit and chat, turning the ringer of your phone off for a period of time, or creating an auto-responder letting people know you will respond to emails within 24 hours)

_____

_____

_____

_____

GOAL SETTING

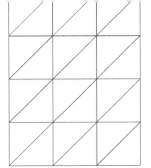

- **MY GOAL IS:**

_____

_____

- **I WILL REACH MY GOAL BY THIS DATE:**

_____

_____

- **IS THERE A DAILY, WEEKLY, OR MONTHLY ACTION I CAN TAKE?**

_____

_____

_____

- **MY ACTION STEP(S):**

_____

_____

_____

- **WHAT WILL REMIND ME TO KEEP MOVING FORWARD?**

_____

_____

The Value
of Banishing Clutter

Are piles in your workspace an avalanche waiting to happen?
There's a lot of value to reducing clutter in your space.
Most of us find we think and function better with clear sur-
faces and only the current project in sight and in mind. Are
you a piler or a filer? How would clearing the clutter benefit you, what could you purge, and where could you start?

■ **HOW CLUTTER AFFECTS ME AND HOW CLEARING IT
COULD IMPROVE MY PRODUCTIVITY:**

_____

_____

_____

■ **WHAT I COULD PURGE TO CLEAR THE CLUTTER:**

_____

_____

_____

■ **WHERE I COULD START TO HAVE THE GREATEST IMPACT:**

_____

_____

_____

GOAL SETTING

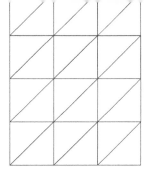

■ MY GOAL IS:

_____

_____

■ I WILL REACH MY GOAL BY THIS DATE:

_____

_____

■ IS THERE A DAILY, WEEKLY, OR MONTHLY ACTION I
CAN TAKE?

_____

_____

_____

■ MY ACTION STEP(S):

_____

_____

_____

■ WHAT WILL REMIND ME TO KEEP MOVING FORWARD?

_____

_____

What's Working and What's Not?

Getting to peak productivity involves evaluation. Having information helps you find the best solutions for you. What's working well and what's not working for you right now? Include some brainstorming on strategies for fixing what's not working.

■ **WHAT'S WORKING?**

_____

_____

_____

_____

■ **WHAT'S NOT WORKING?**

_____

_____

_____

_____

■ **CHANGES I COULD MAKE TO FIX WHAT'S NOT WORKING:**

_____

_____

_____

_____

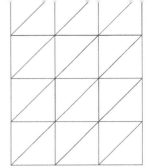

GOAL SETTING

■ MY GOAL IS:

_____

_____

■ I WILL REACH MY GOAL BY THIS DATE:

_____

_____

■ IS THERE A DAILY, WEEKLY, OR MONTHLY ACTION I
CAN TAKE?

_____

_____

_____

■ MY ACTION STEP(S):

_____

_____

_____

■ WHAT WILL REMIND ME TO KEEP MOVING FORWARD?

_____

_____

Overcoming Perfectionism

Perfectionism brings productivity to a screeching halt. It keeps us from moving on to other things because of the belief that something isn't done until it's perfect, yet few things ever are perfect. Perfectionism can also keep you from delegating effectively, since your mindset says, "I am the only one who can do this correctly." Getting beyond that need for perfection will unleash productivity more than you can imagine, and that unleashing comes from insight.

■ **HOW DOES PERFECTIONISM AFFECT YOUR LIFE?**

_____

_____

■ **ARE THERE CERTAIN AREAS OF YOUR LIFE WHERE YOU SEE IT MORE THAN OTHERS, AND WHAT IMPACT IS IT HAVING ON YOUR ABILITY TO BE PRODUCTIVE AND ACHIEVE YOUR GOALS AND DREAMS?**

_____

_____

■ **WHAT MIGHT MAKE IT HARD TO LET IT GO AND ADOPT MORE PRODUCTIVE HABITS?**

_____

_____

_____

_____

GOAL SETTING

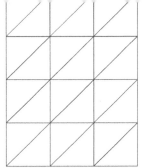

- **MY GOAL IS:**

_____

_____

- **I WILL REACH MY GOAL BY THIS DATE:**

_____

_____

- **IS THERE A DAILY, WEEKLY, OR MONTHLY ACTION I CAN TAKE?**

_____

_____

_____

- **MY ACTION STEP(S):**

_____

_____

_____

- **WHAT WILL REMIND ME TO KEEP MOVING FORWARD?**

_____

_____

HABIT TRACKER

Balance and boundaries are so important to productivity! Making sure you have plenty of time set aside for self-care and creating healthy boundaries that protect your ability to focus on what matters will be key to successfully maintaining healthier habits over time. What habit changes have you made in these areas? What additional changes would you like to make in the future?

■ **HABITS I HAVE CHANGED THAT HAVE HAD A POSITIVE EFFECT ON BALANCE AND BOUNDARIES:**

_____

_____

_____

_____

_____

■ **ADDITIONAL CHANGES I COULD IMPLEMENT:**

_____

_____

_____

_____

_____

MAKE IT A HABIT

Any time you feel overwhelmed and there's too much swirling in your mind, brain dumps are a great tool for getting it all out of your head and in a place where you can organize and process those thoughts. Start with a general list of everything that's swirling in your mind—everything you're worrying about, thinking, or feeling. Then look at the list and determine if there's anything you can or should take action on. Do what you can and leave the rest on the paper—and out of your head.

POWER UP!

Sometimes it's the little things that have a huge positive impact on our days, so find some little things that will do just that. Invest in an app that makes you happy—brings you joy or provides some kind of recharge when you need it—or find a podcast that enhances your life somehow.

Overcoming Procrastination

Do you procrastinate? Do you know why? Maybe you put things off because you fear the end product won't be perfect. Maybe you're too optimistic about the time tasks will take and don't feel a sense of urgency to get started. You might even believe you work best under pressure and have a love/hate relationship with the strain that puts you under. In what ways do you struggle with procrastination, and how does that affect your productivity?

■ **THE WAYS I STRUGGLE WITH PROCRASTINATION ARE . . .**

_____

_____

_____

_____

■ **PROCRASTINATION AFFECTS MY PRODUCTIVITY IN THE FOLLOWING WAYS:**
 (e.g., missing deadlines, increased stress around deadlines, negative mood with things hanging over my head, difficulty concentrating on other projects/things)

_____

_____

_____

_____

GOAL SETTING

■ MY GOAL IS:

_____

_____

■ I WILL REACH MY GOAL BY THIS DATE:

_____

_____

■ IS THERE A DAILY, WEEKLY, OR MONTHLY ACTION I CAN TAKE?

_____

_____

_____

■ MY ACTION STEP(S):

_____

_____

_____

■ WHAT WILL REMIND ME TO KEEP MOVING FORWARD?

_____

_____

Celebrate the Wins

When you're planning the steps and milestones for a big project, don't forget to build in celebrations for each milestone you complete! Celebrations will increase motivation and provide a sense of accomplishment as you keep moving forward. Come up with a list of meaningful and motivating rewards and celebrations you will use as you move through the milestones and tackle the next big project.

■ **MY GO-TO CELEBRATIONS AND REWARDS ARE:** *(Hint: This can be a running list as more ideas come to you!)*

_____

_____

_____

_____

_____

_____

_____

_____

_____

_____

_____

_____

GOAL SETTING

■ **MY GOAL IS:**

_____

_____

■ **I WILL REACH MY GOAL BY THIS DATE:**

_____

_____

■ **IS THERE A DAILY, WEEKLY, OR MONTHLY ACTION I CAN TAKE?**

_____

_____

_____

■ **MY ACTION STEP(S):**

_____

_____

_____

■ **WHAT WILL REMIND ME TO KEEP MOVING FORWARD?**

_____

_____

Give It a Rest

Our mind can only focus for so long before it needs a rest. Working for 90-minute blocks of time and then taking a 5 to 10 minute break is a good way to keep your mind sharp and productivity flowing. Set a timer and your mind will be rested and refreshed for the next task. What could you do to take a mental break between tasks?

■ **TO REFRESH MY MIND BETWEEN PERIODS OF FOCUS, I COULD:** *(e.g., switch environments, get up and walk around, play a quick game on my phone, do some yoga poses)*

_____

_____

_____

_____

_____

_____

_____

_____

_____

_____

_____

_____

_____

GOAL SETTING

■ **MY GOAL IS:**

_____

_____

■ **I WILL REACH MY GOAL BY THIS DATE:**

_____

_____

■ **IS THERE A DAILY, WEEKLY, OR MONTHLY ACTION I CAN TAKE?**

_____

_____

_____

■ **MY ACTION STEP(S):**

_____

_____

_____

■ **WHAT WILL REMIND ME TO KEEP MOVING FORWARD?**

_____

_____

The Value of Collaboration and Support

Collaboration and support open doors to new ideas and even greater growth. Mentors, coaches, and mastermind groups are great sources for both. You may even find you have something to offer others in their journey. What areas of your life or business would benefit from this type of collaboration and support? Are there areas you're struggling in that others might be able to help with? Do you have areas of expertise that could benefit others?

■ **AREAS OF MY LIFE OR BUSINESS WHERE I COULD BENEFIT FROM COLLABORATION AND SUPPORT:**

_____

_____

_____

_____

_____

_____

■ **AREAS OF EXPERTISE I COULD SHARE WITH OTHERS:**

_____

_____

_____

_____

_____

GOAL SETTING

■ **MY GOAL IS:**

_____

_____

■ **I WILL REACH MY GOAL BY THIS DATE:**

_____

_____

■ **IS THERE A DAILY, WEEKLY, OR MONTHLY ACTION I CAN TAKE?**

_____

_____

_____

■ **MY ACTION STEP(S):**

_____

_____

_____

■ **WHAT WILL REMIND ME TO KEEP MOVING FORWARD?**

_____

_____

Reducing Stress

We all experience stress at some time or another. It's good to have strategies for keeping stress from creeping into your days, but it's also important to have strategies for relieving stress. What typically causes stress in your life? What strategies can you use to either keep stress at bay or de-stress when it does occur?

■ **SITUATIONS OR THINGS THAT TYPICALLY CAUSE STRESS IN MY LIFE:**

_____

_____

_____

_____

■ **STRATEGIES FOR AVOIDING STRESS OR RELIEVING IT WHEN IT DOES OCCUR:**

_____

_____

_____

_____

GOAL SETTING

■ **MY GOAL IS:**

_____

_____

■ **I WILL REACH MY GOAL BY THIS DATE:**

_____

_____

■ **IS THERE A DAILY, WEEKLY, OR MONTHLY ACTION I CAN TAKE?**

_____

_____

_____

■ **MY ACTION STEP(S):**

_____

_____

_____

■ **WHAT WILL REMIND ME TO KEEP MOVING FORWARD?**

_____

_____

WEEK

6

DATE

HABIT TRACKER

Thinking back over the changes you have made in terms of habits and behaviors that affect productivity, list the positive changes you have made as they relate to the five roadblocks.

■ **CHANGES I HAVE MADE IN THE AREA OF MINDSET:**

_____

_____

■ **CHANGES I HAVE MADE IN THE AREA OF PLANNING:**

_____

_____

■ **CHANGES I HAVE MADE IN THE AREA OF PRIORITIZING:**

_____

_____

■ **CHANGES I HAVE MADE IN THE AREA OF FOCUS:**

_____

_____

■ **CHANGES I HAVE MADE IN THE AREA OF ENERGY:**

_____

_____

MAKE IT A HABIT

Make time to recharge and refresh a priority in your life and you'll find you have more to give when it's time to get things done.

THROUGHOUT EACH DAY: Work in 90-minute blocks of time, with a 5 to 10 minute break in between.

DURING THE WEEK: Make sure you have one or two days during the week where you are unplugged from the responsibilities and cares of your work week.

VACATIONS: Make sure you take that time to unplug and enjoy the life you're building and fully unwind. It doesn't have to be expensive; just choose something fun, relaxing, and meaningful to you.

POWER UP!

Sometimes a little time off is the best reward, so knock off one hour early or even take the whole day off. It could be today, or you can pick a day, put it on your calendar, and plan something fun that has meaning for you . . . then enjoy that time for yourself!

What Are Your Non-Negotiables?

Does your life currently reflect what you claim to value most?
Are there "non-negotiables" that guide your choices?
Non-negotiables are the values and beliefs you hold so strongly
that you would never make a decision or choose a path that vio-
lates them. Choices become much easier when viewed through
this lens. What are your non-negotiables, and how do you/will you
use them to prioritize the things and people you value most?

■ **MY NON-NEGOTIABLES ARE...**
   *(e.g., family, work, community, staying true to your beliefs, is it
   legal, is it ethical)*

_____

_____

_____

_____

_____

_____

_____

_____

_____

_____

GOAL SETTING

- **MY GOAL IS:**

_____

_____

- **I WILL REACH MY GOAL BY THIS DATE:**

_____

_____

- **IS THERE A DAILY, WEEKLY, OR MONTHLY ACTION I CAN TAKE?**

_____

_____

_____

- **MY ACTION STEP(S):**

_____

_____

_____

- **WHAT WILL REMIND ME TO KEEP MOVING FORWARD?**

_____

_____

Focus on the Right Things

It's been said that failure to plan is planning to fail. A plan will make sure you're focused on the RIGHT things. Where does your focus need to be to get where you want to go in the future? What tasks or activities are most important in your life or business right now? What criteria will you use to determine which tasks and activities deserve your time, energy, and focus in the future?

■ **WHAT AM I FOCUSING ON THAT ISN'T CONTRIBUTING TO MY OVERALL SUCCESS OR GOALS?**

_____

_____

_____

■ **WHAT TASKS AND ACTIVITIES SHOULD I BE FOCUSING ON?**

_____

_____

_____

■ **HOW I WILL DETERMINE WHAT'S IMPORTANT AND WHAT DESERVES MY FOCUS IN THE FUTURE:**

_____

_____

_____

GOAL SETTING

MY GOAL IS:

_____

_____

I WILL REACH MY GOAL BY THIS DATE:

_____

_____

IS THERE A DAILY, WEEKLY, OR MONTHLY ACTION I CAN TAKE?

_____

_____

_____

MY ACTION STEP(S):

_____

_____

_____

WHAT WILL REMIND ME TO KEEP MOVING FORWARD?

_____

_____

Get Organized

Organization is essential to productivity. It keeps you from wasting time looking for something you need. You should always have handy what you need for the current project, and then find a way to neatly store the rest. How organized are you, how does it affect your productivity, and what do you need to be more organized?

■ **WHEN IT COMES TO ORGANIZATION, I AM ...**

_____

_____

_____

_____

■ **IT AFFECTS MY PRODUCTIVITY IN THE FOLLOWING WAYS:**

_____

_____

_____

_____

■ **TO BE MORE ORGANIZED, I NEED ...**

_____

_____

_____

_____

GOAL SETTING

■ **MY GOAL IS:**

_____

_____

■ **I WILL REACH MY GOAL BY THIS DATE:**

_____

_____

■ **IS THERE A DAILY, WEEKLY, OR MONTHLY ACTION I CAN TAKE?**

_____

_____

_____

■ **MY ACTION STEP(S):**

_____

_____

_____

■ **WHAT WILL REMIND ME TO KEEP MOVING FORWARD?**

_____

_____

Healthy Curiosity

Always be curious about what's not working in your life or business, and explore options for improvement. It may seem like something you don't have time for, but ignoring issues can lead to more stress and bigger problems down the road. Reflect on an issue you may have chosen to avoid or ignore in the past. Then reflect on how you would handle a similar situation now more proactively, using all you've learned so far.

■ AN ISSUE I AVOIDED OR IGNORED:

_____

_____

_____

■ WHY DID I AVOID IT?

_____

_____

_____

■ HOW WOULD I HANDLE A SIMILAR SITUATION MORE PROACTIVELY NOW?

_____

_____

_____

_____

GOAL SETTING

■ **MY GOAL IS:**

_____

_____

■ **I WILL REACH MY GOAL BY THIS DATE:**

_____

_____

■ **IS THERE A DAILY, WEEKLY, OR MONTHLY ACTION I CAN TAKE?**

_____

_____

_____

■ **MY ACTION STEP(S):**

_____

_____

_____

■ **WHAT WILL REMIND ME TO KEEP MOVING FORWARD?**

_____

_____

The Value
of Recharging

Looking back over the past seven weeks and the changes you
have made, what changes do you think are making the greatest difference in your productivity? What would you still like to
improve on as you move forward on your path to productivity?

■ **HOW DO YOU FEEL ABOUT TAKING VACATION TIME?**

_____

_____

_____

_____

_____

_____

■ **HOW MUCH VACATION TIME WOULD BE IDEAL TO
YOU AND WHAT WOULD YOUR IDEAL VACATION FOR
RECHARGING LOOK LIKE?**

_____

_____

_____

_____

_____

_____

GOAL SETTING

▣ **MY GOAL IS:**

_____

_____

▣ **I WILL REACH MY GOAL BY THIS DATE:**

_____

_____

▣ **IS THERE A DAILY, WEEKLY, OR MONTHLY ACTION I CAN TAKE?**

_____

_____

_____

▣ **MY ACTION STEP(S):**

_____

_____

_____

▣ **WHAT WILL REMIND ME TO KEEP MOVING FORWARD?**

_____

_____

HABIT TRACKER

Is there something you've always wanted to do or try but thought you didn't have the time or wouldn't be great at it? Pick one of those things and try it. Do it just for the pure enjoyment of trying something new.

▪ CHANGES I HAVE MADE THAT ARE HAVING A POSITIVE IMPACT:

_____

_____

_____

_____

_____

▪ CHANGES I WOULD STILL LIKE TO MAKE:

_____

_____

_____

_____

_____

MAKE IT A HABIT

Honest evaluation gives us the opportunity for improvement and growth, so schedule regular weekly or monthly check-ins with yourself. Focus on what could use improvement and be as honest as possible. Think of it as an empowering exercise, as opposed to a laundry list of failures on your part. Use the insight you gain to look for solutions, then implement those solutions and you will be increasing your potential for success.

POWER UP!

Is there something you've always wanted to do or try but thought you didn't have the time or wouldn't be great at it? Pick one of those things and try it. Do it just for the pure enjoyment of trying something new.

Setting the Stage for Productivity

Does classical music playing in the background spark your creative juices and get you in the zone, or do you work better with complete silence? Would moving your workspace away from a window or getting a more comfortable chair help you stay focused? Understanding what you need in your environment to work your best helps you set the stage for powerful productivity. How do you work best, and what could you do to create a more productive environment?

■ **HOW DO I FOCUS BEST? WHAT TYPE OF ENVIRONMENT ENCOURAGES FOCUS AND PRODUCTIVITY FOR ME?**

_____

_____

_____

_____

_____

■ **WHAT COULD I DO TO CREATE A MORE PRODUCTIVE ENVIRONMENT?**

_____

_____

_____

_____

_____

GOAL SETTING

■ **MY GOAL IS:**

_____

_____

■ **I WILL REACH MY GOAL BY THIS DATE:**

_____

_____

■ **IS THERE A DAILY, WEEKLY, OR MONTHLY ACTION I CAN TAKE?**

_____

_____

_____

■ **MY ACTION STEP(S):**

_____

_____

_____

■ **WHAT WILL REMIND ME TO KEEP MOVING FORWARD?**

_____

_____

Go Back to Your Why

As you go through your days, there may be times you wonder why you're doing what you're doing. When you have those moments, it's always good to go back to your "why," the reason(s) why you do what you do and want the goals you are working toward. Your why was compelling enough to cause you to take action at the start, and it can provide motivation to keep going, even when the going gets tough. So, what is your why?

■ **WHAT'S YOUR WHY?**

_____

_____

_____

_____

_____

■ **WHY IS IT SO IMPORTANT?**

_____

_____

_____

_____

_____

GOAL SETTING

■ MY GOAL IS:

_____

_____

■ I WILL REACH MY GOAL BY THIS DATE:

_____

_____

■ IS THERE A DAILY, WEEKLY, OR MONTHLY ACTION I
CAN TAKE?

_____

_____

_____

■ MY ACTION STEP(S):

_____

_____

_____

■ WHAT WILL REMIND ME TO KEEP MOVING FORWARD?

_____

_____

Do More of What You Love

Working within your strengths and doing more of what you love ignites productivity. You'll feel energized, and naturally accomplish more. Think about all of the tasks and activities that are part of what you do. What do you love doing? What tasks or activities drag you down? How could you do more of what you love and less of what you don't?

■ **WHAT I LOVE DOING:**

_____

_____

_____

_____

■ **WHAT I DON'T LOVE DOING:**

_____

_____

_____

_____

■ **HOW I COULD DO MORE OF WHAT I LOVE:**

_____

_____

_____

_____

GOAL SETTING

■ **MY GOAL IS:**

_____

_____

■ **I WILL REACH MY GOAL BY THIS DATE:**

_____

_____

■ **IS THERE A DAILY, WEEKLY, OR MONTHLY ACTION I CAN TAKE?**

_____

_____

_____

■ **MY ACTION STEP(S):**

_____

_____

_____

■ **WHAT WILL REMIND ME TO KEEP MOVING FORWARD?**

_____

_____

Overcoming Challenges

We all face challenges in our personal and professional lives, and even in our productivity from time to time. Anticipating and planning for challenges you can predict will help you be prepared to overcome them. Do you see any potential challenges to your future progress? Thinking about all you've learned, how will you overcome them?

■ **CHALLENGES I MAY FACE AS I MOVE FORWARD:**

_____

_____

_____

_____

_____

_____

■ **HOW I WILL OVERCOME THEM:**

_____

_____

_____

_____

_____

_____

_____

GOAL SETTING

■ MY GOAL IS:

_____

_____

■ I WILL REACH MY GOAL BY THIS DATE:

_____

_____

■ IS THERE A DAILY, WEEKLY, OR MONTHLY ACTION I
  CAN TAKE?

_____

_____

_____

■ MY ACTION STEP(S):

_____

_____

_____

■ WHAT WILL REMIND ME TO KEEP MOVING FORWARD?

_____

_____

The Art of Scheduling Time

Overbooking and making too many hard commitments causes a lot of stress and puts you in the position of scrambling just to keep up. Evaluate your average day and consider if you're overbooking and making too many hard commitments. Also, are you giving yourself enough flexible time to allow for the unexpected? How could you rearrange your schedule to reduce stress and build in some buffers?

■ A TYPICAL DAY:

_____

_____

_____

_____

_____

_____

■ HOW I COULD REARRANGE MY SCHEDULE TO CREATE MORE FLEXIBILITY AND LESS STRESS:

_____

_____

_____

_____

_____

_____

GOAL SETTING

■ MY GOAL IS:

_____

_____

■ I WILL REACH MY GOAL BY THIS DATE:

_____

_____

■ IS THERE A DAILY, WEEKLY, OR MONTHLY ACTION I CAN TAKE?

_____

_____

_____

■ MY ACTION STEP(S):

_____

_____

_____

■ WHAT WILL REMIND ME TO KEEP MOVING FORWARD?

_____

_____

HABIT TRACKER

How well are you setting the stage for productivity and success? Understanding your why, doing more of what you love and less of what you don't, organizing your time and space to reduce stress, and taking good care of yourself to maximize energy all play a role. Think back on this week's daily prompts, and consider the progress you're making and where you'd still like to improve.

■ **CHANGES I HAVE MADE THAT ARE HAVING A POSITIVE IMPACT:**

_____

_____

_____

_____

_____

■ **CHANGES I WOULD STILL LIKE TO MAKE:**

_____

_____

_____

_____

_____

MAKE IT A HABIT

Cluster similar types of activities so that your time is more stream-lined. For example, if you have several errands you need to run, along with a few appointments for the week, try clustering them all into one or two days. That way, you'll have some days for running and other days for focusing on work that requires "seat time." On your running days, you could even map out a logical, efficient route, so all your running is streamlined, too. It may not always be possible to cluster your to-dos into in-days and out-days, but it's definitely worth the effort if you can.

POWER UP!

What's your favorite reward for celebrating wins? Whatever it is, do it today or in the next few days, and give yourself that well-deserved reward for all your productivity efforts this week!

The Right Tools

Having the right tools for any task will make completing that task more efficient. Most of us have budgets to consider, but think of the expense around getting the tools you need as an investment in you, and be willing to invest! These could be tools for automating things or making your work easier, among other things. How does not having the right tools impact your productivity efforts? What types of tools do you need to boost your productivity and success?

■ **HOW HAVING (OR NOT HAVING) THE RIGHT TOOLS AFFECTS MY PRODUCTIVITY:**

_____

_____

_____

■ **WHAT DO I NEED THAT I DON'T HAVE?**

_____

_____

_____

■ **HOW CAN I BUY, BORROW, OR RENT WHAT I NEED?**

_____

_____

_____

_____

GOAL SETTING

■ MY GOAL IS:

_____

_____

■ I WILL REACH MY GOAL BY THIS DATE:

_____

_____

■ IS THERE A DAILY, WEEKLY, OR MONTHLY ACTION I
   CAN TAKE?

_____

_____

_____

■ MY ACTION STEP(S):

_____

_____

_____

■ WHAT WILL REMIND ME TO KEEP MOVING FORWARD?

_____

_____

Creating Better Email Habits

Managing emails can eat up valuable time. We get a notification and instantly jump over to see who or what it is. We open our inbox and see a full page of new messages we need to read and make a decision on, along with page after page of messages we've left hanging to deal with some other time. It really can be overwhelming! What's the current state of your inbox? How well are you handling emails? How much does your current management of emails affect your productivity throughout the day?

■ **MY CURRENT EMAIL MANAGEMENT SYSTEM IS:**

_____

_____

_____

_____

_____

■ **HOW MY CURRENT EMAIL MANAGEMENT SYSTEM AFFECTS MY PRODUCTIVITY:**

_____

_____

_____

_____

_____

_____

GOAL SETTING

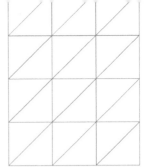

- **MY GOAL IS:**

_____

_____

- **I WILL REACH MY GOAL BY THIS DATE:**

_____

_____

- **IS THERE A DAILY, WEEKLY, OR MONTHLY ACTION I CAN TAKE?**

_____

_____

_____

- **MY ACTION STEP(S):**

_____

_____

_____

- **WHAT WILL REMIND ME TO KEEP MOVING FORWARD?**

_____

_____

Setting Achievable Goals

Sometimes certain things need to happen before a bigger goal can be achieved, like learning a new skill or hiring help. It's important to have short-term goals which are achievable now and long-term goals for the future. Starting with smaller goals—that could lead to bigger goals on the horizon—is a great strategy for achieving the goals you set. Define your bigger goals, then define some smaller goals which will put you on the path.

■ **MY BIGGER GOAL (OR GOALS) WOULD BE:**

_____

■ **MY SMALLER GOALS TO GET ME TO THE BIGGER GOALS ARE:** *(e.g., learning a new skill, completing a certification, increasing revenue so you can hire more people)*

_____

■ **30 DAYS:**

_____

■ **90 DAYS:**

_____

■ **6 MONTHS:**

_____

GOAL SETTING

◼ **MY GOAL IS:**

_____

_____

◼ **I WILL REACH MY GOAL BY THIS DATE:**

_____

_____

◼ **IS THERE A DAILY, WEEKLY, OR MONTHLY ACTION I CAN TAKE?**

_____

_____

_____

◼ **MY ACTION STEP(S):**

_____

_____

_____

◼ **WHAT WILL REMIND ME TO KEEP MOVING FORWARD?**

_____

_____

Doing the Cha-Cha

When you're doing the productivity dance, sometimes "off" days and setbacks break your stride. It happens, and that's okay. It's all about how you view and respond to setbacks. You can choose to see two steps forward and one step back as a cha-cha rather than a failure. Use the prompts below to describe a recent setback (or regression to old habits), how you handled it, and how you could handle it differently in the future to turn it into a positive part of the dance.

■ **RECENT SETBACK OR REGRESSION TO OLD HABITS:**

_____

_____

_____

■ **HOW I HANDLED THE SETBACK:**

_____

_____

_____

■ **TURNING IT INTO A POSITIVE: WHAT CAN/DID I LEARN FROM THAT SETBACK OR MISSTEP?**

_____

_____

_____

_____

GOAL SETTING

- **MY GOAL IS:**

_____

_____

- **I WILL REACH MY GOAL BY THIS DATE:**

_____

_____

- **IS THERE A DAILY, WEEKLY, OR MONTHLY ACTION I CAN TAKE?**

_____

_____

_____

- **MY ACTION STEP(S):**

_____

_____

_____

- **WHAT WILL REMIND ME TO KEEP MOVING FORWARD?**

_____

_____

Managing Life's Challenges

Few things have the power to boost productivity like a positive frame of mind, but problems in our personal lives can sometimes interfere. The more you're able to keep personal problems separate from work, the better. On the other hand, if there is something negative about your situation you can change, it should be dealt with as soon as possible. What's going on in your work or personal life right now, and how does it affect your productivity? Is it something you could or should change?

■ **WHAT'S GOING ON THAT COULD BE AFFECTING MY ABILITY TO HAVE A POSITIVE FRAME OF MIND?**

_____

_____

_____

■ **HOW DOES IT AFFECT MY PRODUCTIVITY?**

_____

_____

_____

■ **IS THIS SOMETHING I CAN CHANGE AND, IF YES, HOW COULD I CHANGE THIS?**

_____

_____

GOAL SETTING

- **MY GOAL IS:**

_____

_____

- **I WILL REACH MY GOAL BY THIS DATE:**

_____

_____

- **IS THERE A DAILY, WEEKLY, OR MONTHLY ACTION I CAN TAKE?**

_____

_____

_____

- **MY ACTION STEP(S):**

_____

_____

_____

- **WHAT WILL REMIND ME TO KEEP MOVING FORWARD?**

_____

_____

HABIT TRACKER

At this point in your journey, you've explored the many ways habits and behaviors can either boost productivity or keep you spinning your wheels. The habits and behaviors that fall within each of the roadblocks have an impact. Compared to where you started, where are you now in terms of Mindset, Planning, Prioritizing, Focus, and Energy?

■ **MINDSET:**

_____

■ **PLANNING:**

_____

■ **PRIORITIZING:**

_____

■ **FOCUS:**

_____

■ **ENERGY:**

_____

MAKE IT A HABIT

Make your inbox less overwhelming by adding some structure and a shift in habits to get it all under control. 1) Unsubscribe from content you're no longer interested in (or those who abuse the privilege of having your email). 2) Create rules and folders. 3) Make immediate decisions the first time you open a message—use the 5 Ds to decide whether you Delete, Delegate, Do it (two minutes or less), Defer for filing (use the folders you create), or Define the action needed and when you will do it. 4) Have an email you use just for online purchases, newsletters.

POWER UP!

Hobbies can be great for helping you unplug from daily stressors, but with all you have going on, you may have been neglecting your favorite hobbies or activities you enjoy. Take some time today to enjoy a hobby or interest that nurtures you—guilt-free and without thinking about to-do lists.

Prime Energy Time

Prime energy time is that part of day where you are at your best. You feel energized and able to get in the zone and get things done. Scheduling tasks that require higher energy for your prime times is a great strategy for rockin' that to-do list. When is your prime energy time, and what tasks could you be scheduling during that time to maximize it?

■ **MY PRIME ENERGY TIME:**

_____

_____

_____

_____

_____

_____

■ **TASKS I COULD SCHEDULE TO MAKE THE MOST OF THAT TIME:**

_____

_____

_____

_____

_____

_____

GOAL SETTING

- **MY GOAL IS:**

- **I WILL REACH MY GOAL BY THIS DATE:**

- **IS THERE A DAILY, WEEKLY, OR MONTHLY ACTION I CAN TAKE?**

- **MY ACTION STEP(S):**

- **WHAT WILL REMIND ME TO KEEP MOVING FORWARD?**

The Feedback Loop You Should Listen To

We all have a built-in feedback loop. Your body will tell you when you're trying to do too much. It *seems* logical to think putting in longer hours will help you get more done, but the truth is, being overworked and run down only lead to stress and health issues, not productivity. How do you know when you're trying to do too much? What cues does your body send, and how well do you pay attention to those cues?

■ **WHAT CUES DOES MY BODY SEND WHEN I'M TRYING TO DO TOO MUCH?**

_____

_____

_____

■ **HOW WELL DO I LISTEN TO THOSE CUES?**

_____

_____

_____

■ **HOW COULD I RESPOND BETTER?**

_____

_____

_____

_____

GOAL SETTING

■ MY GOAL IS:

_____

_____

■ I WILL REACH MY GOAL BY THIS DATE:

_____

_____

■ IS THERE A DAILY, WEEKLY, OR MONTHLY ACTION I
CAN TAKE?

_____

_____

_____

■ MY ACTION STEP(S):

_____

_____

_____

■ WHAT WILL REMIND ME TO KEEP MOVING FORWARD?

_____

_____

Healthy Separation

Technology is great, but not if we allow it to distract us from what matters. With all of the technology at our fingertips, it's harder than ever to unplug and be present in the moment. It's important to be present, both for the people we care about and the things we need to do. How well do you manage the separation from technology to stay focused and be present in the moment? How could you manage it better?

■ **AM I TOO ATTACHED TO TECHNOLOGY? HOW IS MY USE OF TECHNOLOGY AFFECTING MY LIFE OR BUSINESS?**

_____

_____

■ **HOW COULD I MANAGE MY USE OF TECHNOLOGY BETTER?**

_____

_____

_____

_____

_____

_____

_____

_____

_____

GOAL SETTING

■ **MY GOAL IS:**

_____

_____

■ **I WILL REACH MY GOAL BY THIS DATE:**

_____

_____

■ **IS THERE A DAILY, WEEKLY, OR MONTHLY ACTION I
CAN TAKE?**

_____

_____

_____

■ **MY ACTION STEP(S):**

_____

_____

_____

■ **WHAT WILL REMIND ME TO KEEP MOVING FORWARD?**

_____

_____

The Value of
Systems and Processes

Putting systems and processes in place for recurring tasks and activities helps you streamline time and get more done, in less time, with less stress. There are many tools you can use for streamlining email responses, bill paying, marketing campaigns, and many other things, and you'll love the time you save by not having to reinvent the wheel every time those tasks come up. How many things in your life or business could be streamlined by putting processes in place?

■ **WHAT RECURRING TASKS OR ACTIVITIES CAN I SYSTEMIZE OR CREATE A PROCESS FOR TO STREAMLINE MY TIME?**
(e.g., ordering online and using a delivery service for grocery shopping or office needs, doing the books, or paying bills)

_____

_____

_____

_____

_____

_____

_____

_____

_____

_____

GOAL SETTING

■ **MY GOAL IS:**

_____

_____

■ **I WILL REACH MY GOAL BY THIS DATE:**

_____

_____

■ **IS THERE A DAILY, WEEKLY, OR MONTHLY ACTION I CAN TAKE?**

_____

_____

_____

■ **MY ACTION STEP(S):**

_____

_____

_____

■ **WHAT WILL REMIND ME TO KEEP MOVING FORWARD?**

_____

_____

Celebrate, Reflect, Move Forward

Congratulations! You not only successfully worked your way through this process of exploring the roadblocks to productivity and how they affect your life, you've also undoubtedly made some positive changes that are producing great results. Maintaining the changes you adopted will sometimes require daily decisions and effort to keep the momentum going. What changes and progress are you most excited about? What areas are you still struggling in? What can you do to keep the momentum going?

■ **CHANGES AND PROGRESS I AM MOST EXCITED ABOUT:**

_____

_____

_____

■ **AREAS I'M STILL STRUGGLING IN:**

_____

_____

_____

■ **WAYS I CAN KEEP THE MOMENTUM GOING:**

_____

_____

_____

GOAL SETTING

- **MY GOAL IS:**

_____

_____

- **I WILL REACH MY GOAL BY THIS DATE:**

_____

_____

- **IS THERE A DAILY, WEEKLY, OR MONTHLY ACTION I CAN TAKE?**

_____

_____

_____

- **MY ACTION STEP(S):**

_____

_____

_____

- **WHAT WILL REMIND ME TO KEEP MOVING FORWARD?**

_____

_____

HABIT TRACKER

As this part of your productivity journey comes to an end, you have so much to feel good about! Moving forward, remember this journey you embarked on is just that—a journey. There will be new challenges to overcome and new goals to set and achieve. Take a few minutes to express what you're feeling about all you accomplished. Then give some thought to new goals you will set.

■ **HOW I FEEL ABOUT ALL I'VE ACCOMPLISHED AT THE END OF THIS PART OF MY JOURNEY:**

_____

_____

_____

■ **NEW GOALS FOR THE FUTURE:**

_____

_____

_____

_____

_____

_____

_____

POWER UP!

Make it a habit to take a few minutes at the beginning and end of each day to make a list of everything you're grateful for. List all the good things in your life, and don't forget to include those things you might not normally think of as blessings. The struggles and challenges we face teach us valuable lessons. The obstacles we overcome show us how strong we really are. The things we've lost help us appreciate all we still have. There is something to be grateful for in everything, even the lessons we learn from failure. So, let your gratitude shine.

BOOKS

Dweck, Carol S., Ph.D. *Mindset: The New Psychology of Success.* New York: Ballantine Books, 2007.

Morgenstern, Julie. *Organizing from the Inside Out.* New York: Holt Paperbacks, 2004.

Silverstein, Sam. *Non-Negotiable: The Story of Happy State Bank & The Power of Accountability.* Shippensburg, PA: Sound Wisdom, 2015.

Tracy, Brian. *Eat That Frog!: 21 Great Ways to Stop Procrastinating and Get More Done in Less Time.* San Francisco: Berrett-Koehler Publishers, 2017.

Books available at TheProductivityExperts.com/shop:

52 Powerful Success Strategies to Ignite Productivity by Cathy Sexton

7 Points of Impact, a collection of inspirational, motivational, and thought-provoking perspectives from 52 personal coaches, peer advocates, business mentors, and spiritual teachers, including Cathy Sexton

Exploring Productivity, a collection of ideas written by members of the Network for Productivity Excellence, including Cathy Sexton

BLOGS

- The Productivity Experts Blog at TheProductivityExperts.com/blog

APPS

- Focus@Will (FocusAtWill.com). A neuroscience-based music service which helps you focus, reduce distractions, maintain your productivity, and retain information when working, studying, writing, and reading

Acknowledgments

To my husband and daughter, for being the lights of my life and the reason I made the changes that led to my passion for helping others.

To Linda Stroud, my friend, staff, and sounding board, for your tremendous contributions to this project. Thank you for your thought, care, energy, and writing skills. Without you, this and many other projects would not have been finished. Your support of our message on productivity and the work we do enables us to continue to impact many lives in a powerful way. And most importantly, thank you for "getting me" and keeping me true to my vision and brand. You are so important to my success, both creatively and as a source of support.

To my friends, family, and colleagues who continue to love, support, and encourage me in my mission.

About the Author

As a productivity and profit specialist, Cathy Sexton is passionate about helping individuals discover their personal productivity style and accomplish more with less effort. After being diagnosed with a stress-induced life-threatening illness, Cathy set out to reform her workaholic ways and now uses what she learned to help others live healthier, more productive lives. Her business, The Productivity Experts, provides a unique, comprehensive approach to helping business owners overcome the challenges they face. Her ability to get to the heart of what's working and what's not takes businesses from surviving to thriving—fast. Through her speaking, coaching, writing, and programs, she has helped countless groups, individuals, and business owners streamline their processes, get paid what they deserve, and achieve sustainable business growth and success with less stress and more enjoyment of their lives. Cathy can be found at TheProductivityExperts.com.

CPSIA information can be obtained
at www.ICGtesting.com
Printed in the USA
LVHW051031031219
639270LV00004B/7/P